Developing Positive Assertiveness

Third Edition

Sam R. Lloyd

A Crisp Fifty-Minute™ Series Book

This Fifty-Minute™ book is designed to be "read with a pencil." It is an excellent workbook for self-study as well as classroom learning. All material is copyright-protected and cannot be duplicated without permission from the publisher. *Therefore, be sure to order a copy for every training participant through our Web site, www.axzopress.com.*

Developing Positive Assertiveness

Third Edition

Sam R. Lloyd

CREDITS:
VP, Product Development: **Charlie Blum**
Production Editor: **Genevieve McDermott**
Editor: **Luann Rouff**
Production Artists: **Nicole Phillips, Rich Lehl, and Betty Hopkins**
Cartoonist: **Ralph Mapson**

Visit us online at **www.axzopress.com**

Trademarks
Crisp Fifty-Minute Series is a trademark of Axzo Press.

Some of the product names and company names used in this book have been used for identification purposes only and may be trademarks or registered trademarks of their respective manufacturers and sellers.

Disclaimer
We reserve the right to revise this publication and make changes from time to time in its content without notice.

ISBN 10: 1-56052-600-9
ISBN 13: 978-1-56052-600-1
Library of Congress Catalog Card Number 2001086379
Printed in the United States of America

11 12 13 14 13 12

Learning Objectives For:

DEVELOPING POSITIVE ASSERTIVENESS

The objectives for *Developing Positive Assertiveness, Third Edition* are listed below. They have been developed to guide the user to the core issues covered in this book.

THE OBJECTIVES OF THIS BOOK ARE TO HELP THE USER:

1) Improve relationship skills

2) Learn about aggressive, assertive, and nonassertive speech and body language

3) Understand assertive behavior according to personality type

ASSESSING PROGRESS

A Crisp Series **assessment** is available for this book. The 25-item, multiple-choice and true/false questionnaire allows the reader to evaluate his or her comprehension of the subject matter.

To download the assessment and answer key, go to www.axzopress.com and search on the book title.

Assessments should not be used in any employee selection process.

About the Author

Sam R. Lloyd is president of SuccessSystems, Inc., of Boulder, Colorado. He is a past director of the Management Center of Southern Methodist University and has been Assistant Dean of the School of Business at University of Missouri, St. Louis.

For the past 25 years, Mr. Lloyd has trained tens of thousands of individuals in many major organizations, including Motorola, Bristol-Myers Squibb, Hewlett-Packard, Frito-Lay, and Procter & Gamble, among others.

He specializes in assertiveness training, listening skills, interpersonal effectiveness, coaching and counseling, leadership, and customer relations.

Mr. Lloyd is a member of ITAA, ASTD, and SHRM; and is listed in *Who's Who*.

How to Use This Book

This *Fifty-Minute™ Series Book* is a unique, user-friendly product. As you read through the material, you will quickly experience the interactive nature of the book. There are numerous exercises, real-world case studies, and examples that invite your opinion, as well as checklists, tips, and concise summaries that reinforce your understanding of the concepts presented.

A Crisp *Fifty-Minute™ Book* can be used in variety of ways. Individual self-study is one of the most common. However, many organizations use *Fifty-Minute* books for pre-study before a classroom training session. Other organizations use the books as a part of a system-wide learning program—supported by video and other media based on the content in the books. Still others work with Crisp to customize the material to meet their specific needs and reflect their culture. Regardless of how it is used, we hope you will join the more than 20 million satisfied learners worldwide who have completed a *Fifty-Minute Book*.

Preface

This book is for anyone who wants to take charge and live life. Developing positive assertiveness can create personal and professional success and make things happen for you.

Will reading this book result in your being assertive? Not if all you do is read it. If, however, you read and complete the exercises and practice the techniques as recommended, you will learn how to develop assertiveness. This Third Edition includes a helpful new collection of follow-up practice situations in the summary. Completing these exercises over the course of several days or weeks will help you apply and hone your new skills. The book can't make you assertive, but you can!

Developing assertiveness is more than just learning to talk differently. Being assertive requires thinking assertively, feeling confident, and behaving positively. In this book, you will learn how to develop each of these aspects of assertiveness. Explanations of personality and basic psychological concepts will help you gain an understanding about yourself and other people. Guidelines for word choices and behaviors, and numerous exercises, will help you change how you interact with others. Additional exercises will help you change your attitudes that interfere with being assertive.

Assertive people enjoy their work, play, friends, and family. Assertive people are effective, vital, and valued by others. With this book, some personal commitment, and a little time, you can become an assertive person and experience these benefits for the rest of your life.

You can do it!

Sam R. Lloyd

Sam R. Lloyd

Contents

Part 5: Expanding Your Assertiveness

Part 6: Assertive Power Steps

Part 7: Assertive Confrontation

Appendix

Introduction

Assertive Behavior and Why It Is Important

What do you think of when you hear the word *assertive?* Many people think of some-one adamantly standing his or her ground, pushing for his or her own way, refusing to give an inch. Others think of someone who is generally pleasant but stubborn on certain issues. Most people don't understand what assertive behavior really is.

Assertive behavior as defined in this book is a natural style that is nothing more than being direct, honest, and respectful while interacting with others. So what's the big deal? Why is there a need for assertiveness training courses and books? Why do cartoonists poke fun at assertiveness training? Why is there resistance among management in some organizations when assertiveness training is mentioned?

Poking fun and open resistance are symptoms of a lack of understanding. When people do not understand, they are resistant to change. Assertiveness is a most desirable human behavior. It is necessary for honest, healthy relationships. It is the behavior required for "win-win" outcomes in negotiation, conflict resolution, family life, and normal business dealings.

The courses, books, and cassette tapes are necessary because so many people do not understand the desirability and importance of using assertive behavior. As more people develop assertiveness, and begin to influence others, the awareness and acceptance of assertiveness will increase. This book explains why people have to make a conscious effort to develop their assertiveness. Although assertive behavior is natural, it is not the only natural behavior. We humans also use nonassertive and aggressive behavior. These styles create many problems in our relationships, business dealings, and social interactions.

All of us use all three behavior styles throughout our lives. Most of us are not as consis-tently assertive as we might think. As we learn to become more assertive, we reduce our conflicts, failures, dissatisfactions, and stress. Developing assertiveness requires effort, but the rewards are worth it. This book provides you with information, simple directions, and plenty of opportunities to practice becoming more assertive.

After first finding out how assertive you are right now, you will then learn how to identify the three behavior styles previously mentioned: assertive, nonassertive, and aggressive. You will also learn how to ensure successful change, and how to develop positive assertiveness. Once you have learned to develop your assertiveness, you will learn how to maintain the changes you have made. All of this in about 100 pages. Whew!

The first step is to find out how assertive you are now. How assertive are you?

AN ASSERTIVENESS QUIZ

Before learning how to develop your assertiveness, take a few moments to get some idea of where you are right now. Answer the following questions honestly. They will help you gain some insights about your current level of assertiveness. Assign a number to each item using the following scale.

5 = Always   1 = Never

_5_ I ask others to do things without feeling guilty or anxious.

_2_ When someone asks me to do something I don't want to do, I say no without feeling guilty or anxious.

_1_ I am comfortable when speaking to a large group of people.

_5_ I confidently express my honest opinions to authority figures (such as my boss).

_5_ When I experience powerful feelings (anger, frustration, disappointment, and so on), I verbalize them easily.

_1_ When I express anger, I do so without blaming others for "making me mad."

_2_ I am comfortable speaking up in a group situation.

_2_ If I disagree with the majority opinion in a meeting, I can "stick to my guns" without feeling uncomfortable or being abrasive.

_1_ When I make a mistake, I acknowledge it.

_5_ I tell others when their behavior creates a problem for me.

_1_ Meeting new people in social situations is something I do with ease and comfort.

_1_ When discussing my beliefs, I do so without labeling the opinions of others as "crazy," "stupid," "ridiculous," or "irrational."

_8_ I assume that most people are competent and trustworthy and do not have difficulty delegating tasks to others.

_8_ When considering doing something I have never done, I feel confident I can learn to do it.

_5_ I believe that my needs are as important as those of others, and I am entitled to have my needs satisfied.

_40_ Total Score (sum of the 15 numbers)

Turn the page to learn your present level of assertiveness.

HOW ASSERTIVE ARE YOU?

If your total is 60 or higher, you have a consistently assertive philosophy and probably handle most situations well. You may receive some ideas from this book to further improve your skills and effectiveness.

If your total is 45–60, you have a fairly assertive outlook. You are probably naturally assertive in some situations, but this book will help you to increase your assertiveness through practice.

If your total is 30–45, you may be assertive in some situations, but your natural response is either nonassertive or aggressive. Using the suggestions in this book to change some perceptions, and practicing new behaviors, should enable you to handle things much more assertively in the future.

If your total is 15–30, you have considerable difficulty being assertive. If you follow the road outlined in this book, practice and allow yourself time to grow and change, you can become much more comfortable in situations where asserting yourself is important.

How to Develop Positive Assertiveness

2

Three Basic Behavior Styles

It would be great if you could simply decide to go down the road marked "Assertive" and live your life without straying from the path. Real life is full of twists and turns, however, and no one is consistently assertive. All of us use the following three basic behavior styles, depending on the situation and personal factors. The good news is that you can learn to become more assertive more of the time.

1.   Nonassertive

Nonassertive behavior is passive and indirect. It communicates a message of inferiority. By being nonassertive, we allow the wants, needs, and rights of others to be more important than our own. Nonassertive behavior helps create "win-lose" situations. A person behaving nonassertively loses (or is at best disregarded), while allowing others to win. Following this road leads to being a victim, not a winner.

2.   Aggressive

Aggressive behavior is more complex. It can be either active or passive. Aggression can be direct or indirect, honest or dishonest—but it always communicates an impression of superiority and disrespect. By being aggressive, we put our wants, needs, and rights above those of others. We attempt to get our way by not allowing others a choice. Aggressive behavior is usually inappropriate and it violates the rights of others. People who behave aggressively get ahead at the expense of others, and in doing so set themselves up for retaliation. No one likes a bully.

3.   Assertive

Assertive behavior is active, direct, and honest. It communicates an impression of self-respect and respect for others. By being assertive, we view our wants, needs, and rights as equal to those of others. We work toward "win-win" outcomes. An assertive person wins by influence, listening, and negotiating so that others choose to cooperate willingly. This behavior leads to success without retaliation, and encourages open, honest relationships.

BEHAVIOR STYLES QUIZ

Identify the behavior style exhibited by each of the following examples.
Write your answer in the space provided.

NAS=Nonassertive   AS=Assertive   AG=Aggressive

1. _AG_ "Only an idiot would come up with a solution like that! Don't you ever think before you speak?"

2. _NAS_ "You know, maybe we might want to think about a different alternative, uh, what do you think?"

3. _AS_ "Oh, I can't go—I have other plans."

4. _NAS_ "I'm not completely comfortable with your solution. Will you please develop at least one more option?"

5. _AS_ "No, thank you. I appreciate your asking, but I really don't enjoy opera."

6. _AG_ "Opera! You've got to be kidding!"

7. _NAS_ "This probably isn't what you wanted, but I guess I wasn't too sure about what you said, and, anyway, I'm not very good at this kind of thing."

8. _NAS_ "Well, okay, if that's what you want to do."

9. _AS_ "Great idea! Let's do it!"

10. _AS_ "Tracy, please send this to all regional offices today."

Compare your answers to those in the Appendix

Can Behaviors Change?

Do you believe you can't change your basic personality? If so, you and the experts agree. Most experts concur that a general personality type cannot be changed. Once you have developed your basic personality (between ages five and 12), your most natural psychological characteristics do not really change much.

If this is the case, you might ask, "Is it a waste of time to engage in self-improvement?" The answer is no! Even if your core characteristics stay the same, it is possible to change many things about yourself. Things you can change include your beliefs, attitudes, goals, expectations, word choices, and body language. Modestly changing any of these factors can result in your being assertive more often. When this happens, you win!

Before you figure out in which direction you need to travel, it will be helpful if you understand your starting point. Answer the items on the next page (as honestly as you can) to gain a better awareness of your personality characteristics. Your natural response will provide the most accurate insights.

A Personality Quiz

Answer the following questions honestly to determine your starting point.

True False

☐ ☐   1. I usually speak or make eye contact first when encountering another person.

☐ ☐   2. I prefer being with several people, rather than having a one-on-one conversation, in social situations.

☐ ☐   3. I prefer to eat lunch alone.

☐ ☐   4. The best way to make a decision is to assemble all of the facts first.

☐ ☐   5. When I want to have fun, I do something exciting, something with lots of action.

☐ ☐   6. The most important thing in life is having good relationships with family and friends.

☐ ☐   7. When I go to meetings or parties, I spend most of the time talking with one person at a time, rather than interacting with a group.

☐ ☐   8. The best way to learn something is to jump in and do it.

☐ ☐   9. I am very aware of how others respond to me and often worry about whether they like me or if I have displeased them.

☐ ☐ 10. When I make a decision, I trust my intuition—somehow I seem to sense what is best.

☐ ☐ 11. I am usually the one to initiate things, either social activities or business.

☐ ☐ 12. Spending an evening discussing current events, work-related topics, or philosophical issues can be very stimulating and interesting.

☐ ☐ 13. When I am with others, we usually discuss relationships, personal difficulties, or how we feel about our lives.

☐ ☐ 14. My favorite topic is what people have done, where they have been, and what happened. I enjoy telling others about my adventures.

Compare your answers to those in the Appendix

CASE STUDY: PEOPLE-WATCHING

At a professional conference, the following people were observed at the social "mixer" held at the conclusion of the first day. John arrived exactly at the time listed for the event, paused at the entrance of the room to survey the crowd, and purposefully walked to the refreshment area to obtain a drink. After getting his drink, he looked around again and saw someone he knew. Approaching his acquaintance, he made eye contact and said, "Hi, Mary. Have you been here long?" They talked for some time and then John returned to the refreshment area, looking around the room again. Which type is John?

Martha arrived after John. She entered the room and immediately walked toward a group of four people who were nearby. She introduced herself by saying, "Hi everybody. I'm Martha and I'm really enjoying this conference. Are you?" She quickly met everyone and joined in their conversation about the day. Soon the group was sharing information about their families. Martha noticed a friend arrive, smiled, and motioned her friend to come join the group. Which type is Martha?

Sometime later Paula arrived. She had been returning some telephone calls and completing an analysis of a colleague's proposal, as she had promised she would do. When Paula arrived, she paused at the door to see if she recognized anyone. Seeing someone she knew, Paula walked over and the pair spent the entire time in an involved conversation about the problems of world peace. Which type is Paula?

CONTINUED

CONTINUED

Right after Paula entered the room, Bob arrived. He burst into the room, rushed to the refreshment area for a drink, spotted some people he had seen earlier, and walked over to them. Bob said, "Hey, Where's the party? Nothing's happening—let's get something going here!" Within a few minutes, the group left the mixer to go to an area of town where Bob had learned that live entertainment was available.

After finding a nightclub that offered dancing, Bob spent the evening dancing with various members of the group. Which type is Bob?

AUTHOR'S RESPONSE

Easy, isn't it? John is a thinker, Martha is a feeler, Paula is another thinker, and Bob is a doer. All four are successful individuals and lead happy, meaningful lives. They all have different styles and react differently to situations.

To one degree or another, all personality types use all three behavior styles. With better awareness and practice, it is possible to increase assertiveness and decrease nonassertive and aggressive choices. Simply stated, all of us can learn to change.

Ensuring
Successful Change

10

The Five Ps of Successful Change

Any change, large or small, is challenging. For many people, significant change occurs only after some traumatic experience. You don't have to wait for a traumatic event to trigger change, however. You do need to be prepared for change in order to ensure that change will be successful. The following guidelines will help to guarantee any successful changes you wish to make.

1. **Protection.** Change is often scary! Have you ever made a New Year's resolution and failed to keep it? One reason we don't change, even when we truly want to, is fear. Often our fear is vague and unidentified, but it is enough to sabotage making a change. Protection can help you stick with a commitment to change. Here are some protection suggestions:

   ➤ Start your change in your safest environment.

   ➤ Change one thing at a time—slow and easy does it.

   ➤ Whenever you feel unsure or anxious, answer the following questions:

   > *"What's the worst that can happen?"*
   >
   > *"What's the probability that it will happen?"*
   >
   > *"What can I do to prevent it or lower the probability?"*

2. **Potency.** Change is an active process, not a passive one. To activate your personal power, it is necessary to invest some mental effort, emotional involvement, and physical activity to changing. You can learn to tap into your potency if you do the following:

   ➤ Define your change goal in simple, active, positive words.

   ➤ Write your change goal and post it where you see it daily.

   ➤ Imagine yourself practicing your change goal and visualize yourself doing it well.

   ➤ Tell yourself daily, "I can…," "I will…," and "I am…"

3. **Permission.** Each of us requires permission to change. Be sure to give yourself permission, and get permission from significant others in your life who will be affected by your changes. Without their permission and support, you may not succeed.

Tell each person what you plan to do and why. Ask each, "Is that okay with you?" Most significant others will appreciate your consideration of their involvement with your changes. Most will support you when you ask. If someone says no, determine the reason for the reluctance. It might be an important issue to explore and could help you redefine your change goal.

You do not need permission to change from everyone who is important in your life, but having it will ease the pressure on you and normally result in a better support system. Successful people know to accept the help and support of others!

4. **Practice.** Whether learning to ride a bicycle, program a computer, play a musical instrument, or use assertive behavior, an intellectual comprehension of the concepts is not all it takes. (Sorry, all you thinkers!) To become skillful with any behavior requires practice. A great deal of practice may be needed before a new behavior becomes natural and integrated.

➤ Decide what to practice and how it can be best accomplished.

➤ Develop a practice schedule. Be specific about how often, when, and where. Record your efforts.

➤ Allow yourself to make mistakes. Remember: It is practice; you don't have to be perfect!

5. **Proof.** When your practice goes well and you experience satisfaction, you are receiving proof that you can change. This valuable reinforcement encourages you to continue. New behavior must be reinforced repeatedly with positive experiences (proof) to keep the process working and ensure a permanent change.

➤ Ask others to give you positive feedback about your practice.

➤ Give yourself "pats on the back" with positive self-talk.

➤ Establish a practice schedule and reward yourself for keeping your commitment. Give yourself a reward just for practicing. You don't have to be completely changed to deserve some positive reinforcement.

Are You Using the Right Maps?

In the preface of this book, you read that developing assertiveness requires thinking assertively, feeling confident, and behaving positively. In this section, you will learn some ways to change your thinking–attitudes, expectations, beliefs, and perceptions. As long as your thinking is nonassertive or aggressive, you will continue to choose those behaviors. Becoming assertive may require changing how you think about yourself, other people, and life in general.

Practicing new behaviors is an important part of developing your assertiveness. Later, you will receive specific suggestions that will help you practice. Before you begin to practice, however, another important factor requires your attention. Your *expectations* about learning to be more assertive will strongly influence your success.

HOW REALISTIC ARE YOUR EXPECTATIONS?

Complete the following assessment to gain some insight into your expectations, and then check your responses against those of the author.

Write A if you agree with the statement, and D if you disagree.

1. ____ If people know too much about you, they can use this information against you.

2. ____ If everything is going smoothly, look out! Something is bound to go wrong soon.

3. ____ There is a potential positive outcome to any problem or adverse situation.

4. ____ If you want something done right, you must do it yourself.

5. ____ Bad luck comes in threes.

6. ____ When you smile, the world smiles with you.

7. ____ Everyone deserves recognition—not just those who excel.

8. ____ The rich get richer and the poor get poorer.

9. ____ It's okay to admit mistakes—people respect honesty.

10. ____ New people, new situations, and new experiences are fun and exciting.

If you agreed with statements 1, 2, 4, and 5, you are reflecting consistently negative expectations, particularly about people. If you agreed with statements 3, 6, 9, and 10, you have a positive outlook. If you agreed with statement 7, you appear to be generous and realistic. If you agreed with statements 2 and 8, you seem to feel you have little control over life.

Self-Fulfilling Prophecy

Have you ever heard of self-fulfilling prophecy? Self-fulfilling prophecy is experiencing what we expect to experience. It is our getting from others just what we thought we would. It often occurs without our conscious awareness of it. We often succeed or fail because we subconsciously "knew" we would.

Our lives are full of examples of this phenomenon. Have you ever thought, "I'll never get this finished on time!" and then proved yourself right? Have you noticed that some people approach situations with an "I can't do this" attitude and experience problems and failures, while others approach the same situations with an "I can" attitude and succeed? Expectations and attitudes are powerful influences on actual outcomes.

CASE STUDY: SELF-FULFILLING PROHECY

A brilliant young woman named Joyce was leaving home to attend college, but was concerned about her ailing mother. Her mother reassured Joyce, telling her to go and be successful in her college studies. She said, "Don't worry, dear. I'll live to see you graduate!"

Joyce went to college and performed at a superior level the first few years. However, during the first semester of her senior year, she began to experience insomnia and loss of appetite, and struggled with her studies. Her grades fell, but she passed her courses. Her last semester was a disaster. Joyce's health continued to deteriorate and she dropped her two most difficult classes. This required attending another semester before she would graduate.

At the beginning of the next semester, Joyce's friends were concerned about her continued weight loss and general poor health. They encouraged her to seek help. Her doctor could find no explanation for her condition and arranged for her to meet with a psychologist. The psychologist uncovered Joyce's deep concern about her mother. When Joyce's mother pledged, "I'll live to see you graduate," Joyce's subconscious mind interpreted that message as "I will die once you graduate." This simple phrase triggered an unconscious mechanism to delay graduation in order to keep her mother alive.

After counseling, Joyce was able to complete her courses and graduate with honors.

Self-Fulfilling Prophecy (CONTINUED)

Self-fulfilling prophecy is a well-documented phenomenon. Controlled research has shown that teachers, trainers, managers, parents, and so on, influence (often unintentionally) the behavior of their students, employees, and/or children. Every day, subtle messages are delivered that communicate strong expectations.

Expectations, beliefs, attitudes, and values are communicated continuously through words, facial expressions, posture, eye contact, voice tones, and behavior. Without intending to, we influence others and reinforce in them what we expect from them. Thus, we get just what we think we will.

If you expect employees to complain, they will. If you expect them to be trustworthy and hard-working, they will be. It is what you truly expect, not what you say you want, that comes to pass. It is not what you purport to believe in, but what you really believe, that counts. Some managers say they have an "open door," but everyone knows their true message is "don't bother me." Parents may say, "We love you because you're you and a grade of B is fine." However, if Mom and Dad really expect straight As, their message will be communicated regardless of what they say.

How does this relate to being assertive? Assertive behavior comes more naturally when your core philosophy is an assertive one. Whenever your expectations are nonassertive or aggressive, it is easy to send a double message when you wish to be assertive. Is there anything you can do? For openers, you should read the following "Assertive Philosophy" often. Read it with conviction. Say the words aloud as though you sincerely believe them. If you genuinely wish to adopt a more assertive belief system, your perspective will begin to change and you will become more aware of the truth of the statements in your daily experience.

18

AN ASSERTIVE PHILOSOPHY

I recognize that everyone has well-practiced communication habits, and long-standing attitudes that support and defend these habits.

I accept the communication habits of others as fact.

I will offer assertive communication and a "win-win" attitude even when others are offering nonassertive or aggressive styles.

I understand that people change only when they choose to change.

I select my personal standard of communication, rather than react to those of others.

I know others are different from me and that all kinds of people are okay.

I accept responsibility for my feelings, thoughts, opinions, and behaviors. I realize I cannot be responsible for the feelings, thoughts, opinions, and behaviors of others.

I accept that in every relationship, each person has 50% of the responsibility for the success or failure of the relationship.

I know that being nonassertive and aggressive is part of being human.

I know that every assertive choice precludes a nonassertive or aggressive choice and improves the chances for success at work and at home.

Self-fulfilling prophecy has a flip side. When you deliver a speech knowing that people will be interested and amused, sure enough, that's the way you experience it. But if you are anxious about the crowd being bored and unresponsive, you very likely will have a miserable experience.

People who expect negative outcomes (for example, expecting "foreigners" to be inhospitable, expecting to have no fun, dreading the family holidays) invariably have such negative experiences again and again. To create positive outcomes, you must start with positive expectations!

Positive Mental Imagery

When you start practicing the new ways of expressing yourself and handling situations, it is a good idea to also practice the technique of *positive mental imagery*.

Positive mental imagery is using your imagination to visualize yourself saying and doing things successfully and assertively. Envision situations in which you see yourself being assertive. Feel confident, powerful, and effective. Hear your voice sound strong and steady. Experience the satisfaction and pleasure of being assertive.

Do this repeatedly. Do it before you give a business presentation, before you ask an important question, before you introduce yourself to a stranger, and so on. The more powerful your mental image and expectation, the greater the success you should experience.

Remember—only imagine positive outcomes. Don't consider the possibility of things going badly, because your subconscious expectations are so powerful that envisioning failure could undermine your confidence and ultimate success. Recall the example of Joyce, whose subconscious mind kept her from graduating because of a single powerful image planted years earlier.

Use the power of self-fulfilling prophecy to create positive experiences. When you are able to do this, you have begun to develop an assertive philosophy. Think of positive mental imagery as programming a flight plan. Having the right expectations and perceptions before you start your journey is essential if you are going to reach your destination safely.

Programming Yourself for Success

Developing positive mental imagery is an exercise requiring conscious effort. It is a way to influence the subconscious mind. Subconscious expectations and internal dialogues are powerful influences on our perception of reality, our emotions, and our behaviors. Much of what exists in our subconscious was "recorded" in early life and can be thought of as a *psychological program*.

This section explains techniques to change both thinking and feeling patterns to help you become more assertive. You will learn to design a new psychological program that will help support your conscious efforts.

Reprogramming Yourself

Much of our original psychological programming has been with us from childhood and prompts our nonassertive, assertive, and aggressive behaviors. Unlike a computer, which does not have to "unlearn" old habits, a person cannot be totally reprogrammed. While you can't remove your original programming, you can insert some new programming to counteract it.

With people, new programming must be done gradually and the new "program" must be run numerous times before things become automatic. It can be done, however!

How do you know what to put into your program? How do you enter the new programming? Review the quiz items on pages six and 14. These will help you recognize your beliefs, attitudes, perceptions, or expectations that are not consistent with an assertive philosophy. Noticing what you say and do can provide additional examples of behaviors and patterns of speech that are inconsistent with being assertive. Keep a journal in which you record your thoughts and internal dialogue. It will reveal a number of old "programming messages" that you can change to improve your assertiveness.

Create Reprogramming Statements

To create a plan that will help you reprogram yourself, write out new statements that will counteract old behaviors. This plan should include permissions (It's okay to…, I can…), commitments (I will…), and affirmations (I am…). These statements must be written simply, actively, and positively. If they are complex, passive, or negative, you will not get good results.

Start with only a few (four or five) reprogramming statements. Write each statement on a 3" x 5" index card, which is handy to carry with you in a pocket, purse, or briefcase. To use the reprogramming cards most effectively, you should be relaxed. To achieve deep relaxation, you can sit in a hot tub or take a bubble bath, listen to soothing music, rest after exercising vigorously, or meditate. Once relaxed, read each card aloud several times—hear the words, believe them, and let them sink into your relaxed mind.

Inserting ideas into your conscious, but highly relaxed, mind will help you open your subconscious to receive the input. Programs are stored in our subconscious mind, and you must reprogram your subconscious before it can support your new objectives. Read your cards regularly for several weeks to condition your mind. You can read your cards anytime for additional reinforcement, but using the reprogramming routine before sleep is particularly powerful because your subconscious is active periodically during sleep (that's why we dream). Your subconscious will absorb what your conscious mind heard before sleep if you use the routine regularly.

To review, the simple steps to reprogram yourself should include the following:

> ➤ Write simple, active, positive statements that you want to record (one per card).

> ➤ Achieve a state of deep relaxation.

> ➤ Read each statement aloud several times.

> ➤ Sleep and let your subconscious mind absorb the ideas.

> ➤ Do this daily for 21 days.

Your statements should reflect your own objectives and needs. The most important statements are those that will help you change old patterns of thinking and behaving. You are the person best-equipped to identify what you want and need to change, and to create a new program to support this change.

SAMPLE STATEMENTS

Following are some samples of positive reprogramming. You may wish to use these (or others you create) for your initial reprogramming efforts.

It's okay for my wants and needs to be as important as those of others.

- I can get my needs met.

- I will ask for what I want.

- I am someone who deserves having my needs met.

It's okay to have feelings and express them.

- I can express my feelings openly and honestly.

- I will tell others what I am feeling.

- I am an emotionally honest person.

It's okay to make mistakes or not know something.

- I can admit my mistakes or say, "I don't know."

- I will admit my mistakes and say, "I don't know" when appropriate.

- I am honest and will learn from my mistakes.

- I can allow others to make mistakes.

- I will have reasonable expectations of others.

- I am realistic and understand that everyone makes mistakes.

It's okay to trust others.

- I can share and trust.

- I will trust and share.

- I am a trusting and sharing person.

YOUR REPROGRAMMING STATEMENTS

Now that you have the idea, write some simple, active, positive statements for yourself. They can be in any of the following forms. The affirmations (I am...) probably are the most powerful, but your subconscious mind must believe these statements in order for them to work. Using permissions and commitments as a starting point may help.

Permissions:

It's okay to _____

It's okay to _____

It's okay to _____

I can _____

I can _____

I can _____

Commitments:

I will _____

I will _____

I will _____

Affirmations:

I am _____

I am _____

I am _____

Remember, don't use too many statements—only four or five initially. You have plenty of time to expand your behavior modification. Change is more effective one step at a time. This system works if you stick with it and give it an opportunity to work for you.

In addition to reprogramming your subconscious mind each evening, you should also practice the new behaviors you desire on a daily basis. Part 4 will help you learn how to do that.

Feelings:
The Emotional Part
of Assertiveness

26

The Emotions of Assertiveness

Human beings are emotional creatures. All of us have feelings of some sort every waking moment. The emotional component of developing our assertiveness can be one of our most challenging undertakings. One reason for this is because most of us learn lessons about feelings that do not support assertiveness. A few of these lessons are reviewed in this section, and some new ideas are put forth to help you learn to use your emotions as you develop your assertiveness.

One lesson transmitted in our culture is that females are emotional and irrational, and males are unemotional and rational. A true statement? Not really; everyone is emotional. Boys and men often don't learn about emotional honesty because they are taught early that they aren't supposed to be emotional. Girls and women often learn exaggerated emotional responses to situations because they are expected to be emotional.

Another myth most of us grow up believing is that people can make each other feel. For example, do you believe that you can make someone angry? Do you worry about being assertive and "hurting someone's feelings?" This myth teaches us to believe that our words and actions literally cause other people to feel the emotions they feel. It teaches us to believe that we have no choice about our own feelings. It also teaches us to believe that we are responsible for one another's feelings.

Why is it called a myth? Because it is not true! Feelings are a choice. Although most people don't believe that when they first hear it or read it, further explanation may help you understand the truth of that statement.

Cause and Effect

One way to understand that feelings are a choice is to think about cause and effect. If words, actions, or events make someone angry, frightened, or sad, that person has no choice. The person is made to feel that feeling. The word, action, or event is the cause, and the feeling is the effect. If the process truly were a cause-and-effect process, wouldn't it make sense that the same cause would then produce the same effect (feeling) in everyone? Simple observation proves that different people have different feelings about exactly the same event. Therefore, it is the person experiencing the words, actions, or events who chooses an emotional response.

Example: If someone decided to surprise you for your birthday by hiring someone in a clown suit to show up at your place of work and sing a song for you, how would you feel about the surprise? Whatever feeling you might have, you would probably agree that other people would respond differently to the same surprise. Some would be delighted and happy, others would feel embarrassed, others might get angry, and some might be disappointed. There is no sure way to predict anyone's emotional response in advance.

Granted, your emotional choice may be a strong habit. You might experience the same feeling in response to the same stimulus every time. Although you might perceive the process as being "made to feel," you could in fact choose a different emotional response, even though it might feel unnatural at first.

Assertiveness demands emotional honesty. This is difficult to accomplish if you will not accept responsibility for your own feelings.

The ABC Process

Another way to understand that we determine our feelings is to examine the process as an A, B, C system:

> **A = Stimulus (word, behavior, event, etc.)**
>
> **B = Internal dialogue or self-talk**
>
> **C = Emotion**

This whole process may happen in less than a second, but all three steps are always involved whenever we have an emotional response to something. Often it will seem as if the feeling occurs simultaneously with the stimulus, but in a fraction of a second there was a sequence from A to C.

CASE STUDY: SPECIAL DELIVERY

Example: While working in his office, a man is interrupted by the delivery of an overnight letter. He glances at the sender's address and notices that it is from the city where his ex-wife lives. Immediately he feels anger and throws it on his desk saying, "Why can't she just stay out of my life and let me live in peace!?"

Did the overnight letter make him angry? Many people would answer yes. Obviously, he wasn't angry before he received the letter and he got angry when he looked at it. Of course it made him angry.

What really happened was the A, B, C process. The man noticed the city of origin (A); assumed that the letter was from his ex-wife and that it contained some unwanted intrusion on his life (B); and then felt angry (C). His anger was in response to his thoughts. He could just as easily have felt guilty, sad, anxious, or pleased.

To continue the story, the man opened the letter. As soon as he read it, he whooped loudly, started laughing, jumping up from the desk, and did an impromptu dance around his office. Why the sudden change in emotion?

The letter was from a client. The message was as follows: "Our board met today and considered your proposal. Thought you would like the news as soon as possible. We like your ideas and will double our business with you starting next month."

Upon reading this message (A), the man thought about a trip to Hawaii and how much praise he would receive from his boss (B), and became very happy (C). It was the same letter about which he first felt angry! The letter did not make him mad or glad. His self-talk influenced his choice of feelings.

Another important reason for understanding the truth about feelings is to learn to use more of your power. By allowing others to "make you feel," you give your power to others. The old saying "Sticks and stones may break my bones, but words can never hurt me" has an element of truth. Know that when you feel hurt, embarrassed, angry, sad, or joyful in response to the words of others, you are choosing those feelings.

Choice and Win-Win Relationships

Assertiveness is a win-win approach and philosophy. To build and maintain win-win relationships, each person must accept responsibility for his or her own feelings, thoughts, and behaviors. You cannot be solely responsible for the feelings of others because you do not "make them feel." You are responsible for what you say and do because your words and actions invite others to feel certain emotions. Whether they do or not is up to them!

Assertiveness requires us to accept responsibility for our thoughts, feelings, and behaviors; and requires us to respect the thoughts, feelings, and behaviors of others. When an individual accepts these responsibilities and stops blaming others for his or her feelings, a giant step has been taken toward a win-win philosophy.

WHAT FEELING WOULD YOU CHOOSE? WHY?

In the following exercise, read the situation (**A**) and write your spontaneous emotion in the space under (**B**). Once you identify your feeling, write in what your self-talk was under (**C**).

Situation (A)	Feeling (B)	Self-Talk (C)
A driver changes lanes without warning and almost hits your car.	_____	_____ _____
You are asked spontaneously by your boss to come forward at a company meeting and explain a project to 100 people.	_____	_____ _____ _____ _____
You finish an important presentation for your boss and important clients. When you return to your seat, a colleague tells you that your shirttail/blouse is showing through an open zipper.	_____	_____ _____ _____ _____ _____

CONTINUED

WHAT FEELING WOULD YOU CHOOSE? WHY?

Whatever feelings and self-talk you experienced for these situations are okay. There is nothing "bad" about feeling angry, embarrassed, or elated. Your responses might not be the most productive or logical for the situation, but feelings are not logical. To change how you respond to certain situations, begin by changing your internal dialogue.

To practice learning new emotional responses by changing your self-talk, use the same situations from the preceding exercise but create some different self-talk that will help you have a positive feeling.

Situation	New Self-Talk	Resulting Positive Feelings
Near accident	_____	_____
	_____	
Speaking to 100 people.	_____	_____
	_____	
Open zipper.	_____	_____
	_____	

Talking About Feelings

An important part of developing assertiveness is expressing your honest emotions. Many people don't do that. Even if you understand that being emotional is okay and part of being human, you may need practice to talk about your feelings. The assertive way to express feelings is to say, "I feel…," "I'm feeling…," "I am…," "I was…," and "I get…" What follows each phrase is a word or words describing a feeling.

First, you must know what you are feeling. To figure out which emotion you are experiencing, ask yourself, "What am I feeling—mad, sad, glad, or scared?" Those are the four basic human emotions, and this is a good question to help you get in touch with your feelings quickly and accurately. Some feelings are combinations of two or more of the four categories.

The following table may help you develop a vocabulary of emotions as you learn to express your feelings in a direct, open, and honest manner.

mad	sad	glad	scared	combination
irritated	unhappy	pleased	anxious	guilty
annoyed	disappointed	happy	worried	jealous
angry	despondent	joyful	fearful	frustrated
ticked off	blue	delighted	concerned	embarrassed
furious	hurt	effervescent	afraid	uncomfortable
miffed	grief	comfortable	nervous	confused
upset	down	up	inhibited	perplexed
chapped	lonely	excited	uncertain	torn

You can add to the lists. Because each person chooses and experiences feelings in a unique way, some feeling words fit into different categories. Some people use "upset" to mean mad, while others use it to mean sad. You decide which words best reflect your feelings.

DEVELOPING EMOTIONAL AWARENESS

For the next week or two, when you feel an emotion, stop and ask yourself, "What am I feeling—mad, sad, glad, scared?" When you identify your feeling, make yourself aware of the underlying self-talk associated with it. Learn to recognize the physical symptoms related to that feeling. What signals accompany anger, fear, sadness, and joy? Recognizing these physical clues will help you increase your emotional awareness. This is the first step toward expressing your feelings assertively.

In the next section on behavior, you will learn more about word choices to express not only your feelings, but also your opinions and thoughts, facts, and so on. Also provided are guidelines for assertive behavior that will reinforce your assertive words.

P A R T 4

Changing Your Behaviors

Choosing Assertive Words Carefully

Now that you have an understanding about how to change your thinking and feeling patterns, you need some information about changing your behavior.

To communicate thoughts, feelings, and opinions assertively, you need to choose words that are direct, honest, appropriate, and respectful. Some words simply do not fit these criteria and therefore cannot be delivered assertively. Words are only one aspect of being assertive, but you must use assertive words if you are to be assertive with others.

Guidelines for Assertive Word Choice

Use "I" statements, rather than "you" statements.

Compare the following:

> *"You always interrupt my stories!"* (Aggressive)
>
> *"I would like to tell my stories without interruption."* (Assertive)

Use factual descriptions instead of judgments or exaggerations.

Compare the following:

> *"If you don't change your attitude, you're going to be in real trouble."* (Aggressive)
>
> *"If you continue to arrive after 8:00 a.m., I will be required to place you on two days' probation without pay."* (Assertive)

Express thoughts, feelings, and opinions reflecting ownership.

Compare the following:

> *"He makes me angry!"* (Denies ownership of feelings)
>
> *"I get angry when he breaks his promises!"* (Assertive and owns feelings)
>
> *"The only sensible policy is to match the competition."* (States opinion as fact; aggressive, controlling)
>
> *"I believe matching the competition is the best policy."* (Owns opinion; assertive)
>
> *"Don't you think we should table this for now?"* (Passive, indirect, denies ownership)

Use clear, direct requests or directives (commands) when you want others to do something, rather than hinting, being indirect, or presuming.

Compare the following:

> *"Would you mind taking this to John?"* (Indirect, only inquires about willingness)
>
> *"Will you please take this to John?"* (Assertive request)
>
> *"Please take this to John."* (Assertive directive)
>
> *"Why don't you stop on the way home and pick up milk?"* (Indirect, encourages the other to think about *not* doing it)
>
> *"Will you please pick up milk on your way home?"* (Assertive request)
>
> *"Please pick up milk on your way home."* (Assertive directive)

Being Direct and Honest

People avoid being direct and honest because they have learned it is impolite or pushy. Unfortunately, while attempting to avoid being inappropriate, we sometimes choose words that communicate a lack of respect. Sometimes we are so "careful" we don't communicate the real message.

When we say "Don't you think…" instead of "I think," we are communicating indirectly. If you really listen to the words, they sound condescending. When you ask, "Why don't you…" instead of "Will you," you are literally asking a person to find reasons not to. When you say, "I need…," and presume someone will take care of your needs, you communicate a lack of respect or an air of superiority. If you say "I need" or "I want," learn to add a request or directive in order to be assertive.

These may seem like picky details. You might say, "Most people know what is meant when I use those words, so what's the difference?" The difference is that you may be getting expected results only because people are able to figure out your unexpressed intentions. You may not be getting their respect. Continuing to use improper wording reinforces old habits and interferes with your being truly assertive. You can increase your success rate and improve relationships by using the direct, honest, assertive words.

SOME DO'S AND DON'TS

Following are some do's and don'ts for assertive word selection.

Do

➤ Say no politely and firmly

➤ Express feelings honestly

    say "I'm angry"; "I'm disappointed"; "I'm delighted"; "I enjoy being with you"

➤ Be realistic, respectful, and honest

    say "This is the third straight month your report has been late."

    say "Thank you for asking. I prefer no smoking in my car."

➤ Express preferences and priorities

    say "I don't have a particular movie to suggest. I do want to avoid ones with violence."

Don't

➤ Don't say "I can't" or "I won't be able to."

➤ Don't depersonalize feelings or deny ownership, by saying:

"You make me mad"; "That's disappointing"
"That's delightful"; "You make me feel so good"

➤ Don't exaggerate, minimize, or use sarcasm, by saying:

"You are never on time with your reports."
"Uh, okay, we wouldn't want to strain your will power!"

➤ Don't defer to be sociable or agree unwillingly, by saying:

"I don't care—whatever everyone else wants is okay with me."

TIME TO PRACTICE

With the preceding guidelines fresh in your mind, write an assertive response that is appropriate for the following situations:

1. You did not understand what someone just told you and want her to restate her message.

    _____

    _____

2. You believe you deserve a raise and decide to ask your boss directly.

    _____

    _____

3. You have been invited to a social event that does not interest you. Decline the invitation.

    _____

    _____

4. You are pleased about what someone has done. Tell him or her your feelings.

    _____

    _____

Do a quick self-check by asking yourself, "What do these words invite from the other person?" This will help you determine if your words are assertive, aggressive, or nonassertive.

Body-Language Signals

You have now seen that your choice of words is critically important. Perhaps even more essential is *how* you say them. Your delivery of the message makes all the difference. Most people use the phrase *body language* to refer to all aspects of interpersonal communication beyond the choice of words. Everything becomes important when a message is being delivered: voice tone, volume, inflection, pace, eye contact or lack of it, facial expression, gestures, movements or lack thereof, posture, muscle tension, changes in skin coloring, clothing, hair style, eyeglasses, and so on. Whew!

Staying continuously aware of all aspects of body language is not possible. Having some awareness is very important in your assertiveness training. Even though other people might not be able to list all of your body-language signals during an interaction, they respond and interpret them unconsciously as part of receiving your message. This process is automatic, constant, and complex.

Don't be discouraged. You don't have to constantly monitor all aspects of body language to be assertive. You do, however, need to accompany your words with some body-language signals that will help you be perceived as an assertive person. Perfection is not required for success.

On the next page are some basic body-language signals that have been categorized according to how most people perceive them. As you read through the lists, you may want to act out each one to get a better sense of what the signal communicates.

NONASSERTIVE	ASSERTIVE	AGGRESSIVE
Posture		
• slumped • shoulders forward • shifting often • chin down • sitting: legs entwined	• erect but relaxed • shoulders straight • few shifts, comfortable • head straight or slight tilt • sitting: legs together or crossed	• erect, tense, rigid • shoulders back • jerky shifts or planted in place • chin up or thrust forward • sitting: heels on desk, hands behind head or tensely leaning forward
Gestures		
• fluttering hands • twisting motions • shoulder shrugs • frequent head nodding	• casual hand movements • relaxed hands • hands open, palms out • occasional head nodding	• chopping or jabbing with hands • clenched hands or pointing • sweeping arms • sharp, quick nods
Facial Expression		
• lifted eyebrows, pleading look, wide-eyed, rapid blinking • nervous or guilty smile • chewing lower lip • shows anger with averted eyes, blushing, guilty look	• relaxed, thoughtful, caring or concerned look, few blinks • genuine smile • relaxed mouth • show anger with flashing eyes, serious look, slight flush of color	• furrowed brow, tight jaw tense look, unblinking glare • patronizing or sarcastic smile • shows anger with disapproving scowl, very firm mouth or bared teeth, extreme flush
Voice		
• quiet, soft, higher pitch • uhs, ahs, hesitation, stopping in "midstream" • nervous laughter • statements sound like questions, with voice tone rising at the end	• resonant, firm, pleasant • smooth, even-flowing, comfortable delivery • laughter only with humor • voice tones stay even when making statement	• steely quiet or loud, harsh • "biting off" words, precise, measured delivery • sarcastic laughter • statements sound like orders or pronouncements

NONASSERTIVE, ASSERTIVE, OR AGGRESSIVE?

Given the list of body-language signals on the previous page, how would you classify the following?

NAS = Nonassertive   AS = Assertive   AG = Aggressive

1. _____ Elbows out, fists on hips

2. _____ Touching someone's forearm as you speak with them

3. _____ While walking, putting an arm around someone and firmly grasping their shoulder

4. _____ Shifting repeatedly from one foot to the other while standing

5. _____ Constantly nodding head up and down

6. _____ Leaning back, propping feet on desk, grasping hands behind head

7. _____ Looking at toes while speaking

8. _____ Leaning forward with hands grasped, elbows on knees while seated facing someone

9. _____ Rapidly tapping pencil (like a drumstick) while listening

10. _____ Sitting with elbows on table, hands together, chin on hands while listening

11. _____ Standing with arms folded while listening

12. _____ Standing with arms folded, head tilted, and legs crossed

13. _____ Looking over the tops of eyeglasses

14. _____ Twirling a pencil with fingers at each end while talking

15. _____ Elbows on table, hands together at fingertips forming a "steeple"

Compare your answers to those in the Appendix.

Body-Language Signals (CONTINUED)

It is important to understand that body-language signals have many possible interpretations. A single body-language cue is often not enough for an accurate "reading" of the communication. Body-language signals must be interpreted in total. Much like a detective, it is necessary to discover and interpret a number of clues to solve the body-language mystery.

One way to become more sensitive to body language is to become a "people watcher with a purpose." This can help you develop a better awareness of how body language communicates nonassertive, assertive, and aggressive behaviors. You will notice that people not only use different words with each style, but also communicate these styles with their body-language signals. Recognizing nonassertive and aggressive signals can help you learn to avoid using them when your goal is to be perceived as assertive.

One way to develop your assertiveness is to find an assertive person and observe his or her behavior. Take note of the words and body language the person uses. Most of what we learned as children was learned through observation. The system still works. Following a good role model is an easy and fun way to learn how to become more assertive.

CASE STUDY: BODY LANGUAGE WINS

Jurors are often influenced by the body language of the opposing attorneys and witnesses. In a recent personal injury case, the attorney representing the plaintiff strutted, smirked, and used a loud, nasal toned voice while questioning witnesses. When the defense attorney would comment or ask questions, the plaintiff's attorney would make disbelieving or disapproving facial expressions.

The defense attorney was not a strong personality. He spoke in a quiet voice. He slumped when he sat and walked with poor postures. His movements were jerky and uncertain.

The jury seemed offended by the behavior of the plaintiff's attorney. On the other hand, they were not impressed with the defendant's attorney. Without knowing any of the evidence in the case, can you predict which attorney won?

Obviously, the evidence and testimony were factors; however, the consistently obnoxious behavior of the plaintiff's attorney was the key factor. The jurors were so annoyed by his aggressiveness toward the witnesses that they decided for the defense. A respectful, assertive attorney could have won for the plaintiff.

Stop Signs and Green Lights

Stop Signs

Several signals will indicate when you are headed down the wrong road. These signals can be either nonassertive or aggressive. Read and learn the signals. Practice using what you learn. It's okay to stop and say something like, "Excuse me. Let me start over." Others will respect your efforts to be assertive.

STOP Saying "You should…," "You must…," "You have to…" Restate as either a request or directive.

STOP Using exaggerated words: "obviously," "absolutely," "always," "never," "impossible." Restate with more realistic and factual words.

STOP Saying, "You know," "maybe," "kinda," "sorta," "only," "just," "I guess." Restate in a more direct, confident manner without the wishy-washy qualifiers.

STOP Asking, "Can you…, "Could you…," "Would you…," "Why don't you…," "Would you mind…," "Do you think you might…" Request by asking, "Will you please…"–it is the only question that truly asks for action and a commitment!

STOP Using "it," "that," "one," "you," or "we" instead of "I." State your thoughts with, "I think…"; your opinions with "I believe…"; and your feelings with, "I feel… (mad, sad, glad, scared)" or "I am… (mad, sad, glad, scared)."

Green Lights

The following signals indicate that you are on the right road, communicating assertively. Keep going when you have green lights!

GO When you feel relaxed, comfortable, and stress free. These are positive signs that you are being assertive.

GO When the person with whom you are interacting displays attentiveness, comfort, cooperation, and respect. When you see no signals of bad feelings, rebellion, disregard, or defensiveness, you are being assertive.

GO When another says, "okay," "sure," or "I'll be glad to" in response to your request or directive. When others do what you want with no indication of resentment or discomfort, you have good evidence you were assertive.

GO When others are assertive with you. When they communicate their honest thoughts, feelings, opinions, wants, and needs in a direct and respectful manner, they are affirming your assertive behavior with them.

Expanding Your Assertiveness

Four Assertive Styles

Everyone has a natural assertive style that comes from his or her basic personality. You probably will recognize yours among the following four descriptions:

Supporting/Caring

This style communicates warmth, nurturing, and concern for others. Content is presented in a direct, honest, and respectful manner. It maintains an awareness of the feelings of others. Those who naturally use this assertive style are often *feelers*.

Directing/Guiding

This is an impersonal style that communicates a no-nonsense, authoritative approach and a concern for results. It is a firm, but respectful style using directives, rather than requests. It does not come across as being bossy or dictatorial. The directing/guiding style communicates beliefs and opinions appropriately, as well as commands. Those who use this style most frequently are *doers* and/or *thinkers*.

Analytical

This style also is impersonal and matter-of-fact. It communicates facts, information, thoughts, and probabilities. This style uses requests to obtain results, rather than directives. Directing/guiding is a "tell 'em" style, whereas Analytical is an "ask 'em" style. Analytical is calm and emotionless. It is used most naturally by those in the thinker group.

Expressive

This style is animated, energetic, spontaneous, and emotional. Feelings, likes and dislikes, wants, and needs are communicated in this style in an open and expressive manner. Those using this style are usually intuitive, creative, spontaneous, and lively. They are normally *doers* or *feelers*.

Did you recognize your natural assertive style? Did you recognize others you know as you read each description? All four styles are assertive because each communicates in an appropriate, direct, and honest manner.

WHICH STYLE IS WHICH?—A QUIZ

Using the abbreviations listed below, identify which assertive style is used in the following examples. Reading them aloud may help you recognize the differences.

S/C= Supporting/Caring   D/G = Directing/Guiding
A = Analytical   E = Expressive

1. _____ "The quarterly report indicates a 7% increase in productivity."

2. _____ "Hey! That's terrific!"

3. _____ "I really appreciate your summarizing all that data for us."

4. _____ "It's important to nail down just how that was accomplished."

5. _____ "Give me some more details on that new product line."

6. _____ "I know you're excited about our new products, Pat, and I would like to hear more about them after we finish the productivity discussion."

7. _____ "Thank you Terry. I estimate about 20 minutes will be required to complete the productivity analysis. The next item on the agenda will be new products."

8. _____ "Okay, let's do it. This productivity stuff is boring and I'd like to get on to a new topic!"

9. _____ "Chris, you sure like the new ideas, don't you? Thank you for being patient and keeping a lid on long enough for us to finish."

10. _____ "My analysis revealed three factors that contributed to the productivity improvement. The first was…"

Compare your answers to those in the Appendix

CASE STUDY: WORKING TOGETHER

Leann, a manager with a directing/guiding style, had an administrative assistant, Sue, who had a supporting/caring style. Sue wanted to help Leann and was dedicated to doing everything possible to maintain a satisfying relationship. Leann was unconcerned about the quality of their relationship and concentrated more on getting things done.

Over time, Leann's continued use of directives began to create stress for Sue. Like most people with the supporting/caring style, Sue interpreted commands as uncaring and occasionally heard them as reprimands. Sue's interest in Leann's family and home life seemed unprofessional to Leann and was a source of discomfort.

After months of working together, Sue resigned. In the exit interview conducted by the personnel director, Sue explained that her manager seemed to disapprove of her many efforts to help. Sue said she was leaving to find a job with a boss who would appreciate qualities such as loyalty, devotion, and anticipation of needs.

When the personnel director reviewed the interview with Leann, the result was amazed perplexity. Leann explained how her assistant always wanted to talk about family life and seemed to hover about, expressing concern about not being able to help more. "I don't like someone fussing over me all the time," Leann explained. "I want my employees to do what I tell them and concentrate on doing their work."

Working Together (CONTINUED)

It is obvious to an informed observer how the manager and assistant failed to understand each other's priorities and style. When those involved don't know about differences in personality styles, they often fail to communicate and experience stressful relationships.

By learning to recognize and use the four assertive styles, you will be able to communicate more effectively with almost everyone. Once you recognize a style and sensitively match it (at least part of the time), you will improve your communication with that person—even if it was previously difficult to make a connection. An easy way to remember the importance of matching styles is to think of speaking with someone via short-wave radio. If you send your message to one channel and she receives it on another channel, you will not be able to communicate. When you are both on the same channel, you can communicate.

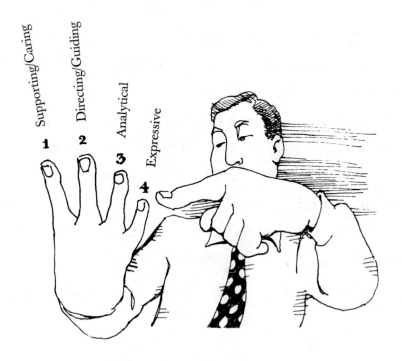

Sending Assertive Messages

The following exercise enables you to practice sending messages in different styles. Write your responses to these situations and then compare them with the samples provided. *Don't look at the samples before writing your message.* The purpose of this exercise is to practice using what you have learned. If you need help, look at the examples at the beginning of the chapter. Your words do not have to be the same—but the meaning should be similar.

Tell or ask Pat to assist you with a project.

Supporting/Caring style: _____

_____

Directing/Guiding style: _____

_____

Analytical style: _____

_____

Expressive style: _____

_____

Give Chris feedback about how well she has organized a meeting.

Supporting/Caring style: _____

_____

Directing/Guiding style: _____

_____

Analytical style: _____

_____

Expressive style: _____

_____

Compare Your Responses

Compare your messages with the following example responses. Yours may not be exactly like the samples, but they should help you judge how successfully you were able to "switch channels." Remember: It is not simply your choice of words that creates a style. Read your messages aloud with appropriate delivery to help you communicate in the different styles.

Pat:

Supporting/Caring: "Pat, if you can spare the time, will you please give me some help on this project? Thank you so much."

Directing/Guiding: "Pat, please complete this part for me so I can wrap up this project."

Analytical: "Pat, if you assist me, I can complete the project this week. Will you organize this section?"

Expressive: "Pat! Help! I'm swamped—how about running some figures for me?"

Chris:

Supporting/Caring: "Chris, I really appreciate how well you organized the conference. Everyone seemed comfortable with the arrangements."

Directing/Guiding: "Chris, that was a fine job you did on the meeting arrangements."

Analytical: "Chris, your arrangements for the conference were very complete. The sessions were on time, everyone had all the necessary information, and the meeting ran efficiently."

Expressive: "Super job, Chris! Great meeting!"

CAN YOU IDENTIFY THESE PEOPLE?

Two business people were seated in the same row on an airplane. The middle seat was initially empty. It was a full flight and a third person finally occupied the seat between the two travelers. The person in the middle also appeared to be traveling for business.

The person by the window asked the traveler in the middle, "What is your destination?" The passenger answered, "Chicago." After a short while the passenger by the window asked, "What business are you in?" The reply, "Electronics." The person by the window made no further attempts to communicate.

The person sitting in the aisle seat heard the preceding interaction. This passenger also noticed the middle passenger's expensive suit, costly wrist-watch, and eel-skin briefcase. Assessing the visual clues and lack of responsiveness to the other person's questions, the aisle passenger said to the traveler in the middle seat, "Tell me about what you do." At that, the traveler launched into a lengthy explanation of his business, the purpose of the trip, and his past successes!

1. **Which communication style was used by the window-seat passenger?**

    _____

2. **Which style was used by the aisle-seat passenger?**

    _____

3. **What was the middle passenger's personality type (thinker, feeler, or doer)?** _____

Compare your answers to those in the Appendix.

HOW DELIVERY AFFECTS DIFFERENT STYLES

How you say words is important when using each style. Following are some suggestions for successful delivery:

Supporting/Caring.

Use a warm, nurturing, mellow tone of voice. Communicate personal interest, appreciation, concern, gratitude, or empathy by making good eye contact and using comforting facial expressions. (Think of a loving grandparent.)

Directing/Guiding.

Be firm and authoritative, but not harsh or dictatorial. Your delivery should be matter-of-fact, direct, and serious. Facial involvement is an expression of concentration or purpose.

Analytical.

Use an even, no-nonsense, pragmatic delivery. Your facial expression should be alert and thoughtful. You can be polite, but not emotional.

Expressive.

Everything is expressive! Your voice range and facial expressions are almost limitless. Be animated with your face, hands, and body movements. Show emotion.

Role models can help you learn to use all four assertive styles. As mentioned earlier, it is fun to follow the example of someone whose natural style is one of the four assertive styles. It is very likely that you have mentally identified someone with a similar style to each of the types described. If not, you should be able to find one of each by listening and observing. It is also possible to find examples of the four assertive styles in television programs or movies. Once you find a role model of the style you want to practice, study that person and adopt those characteristics that seem most effective.

Identifying Styles to Enhance Communication

To identify people who fit into one personality group or the other, look for the characteristics described below. Once you have figured out what someone's dominant personality type is, you can communicate more effectively with that person by using the matching assertive style.

Supporting/Caring

These people value relationships and work hard at maintaining them. They often do thoughtful things, showing an awareness of, and a concern for, others. They are comfortable with self-disclosure and will talk about personal issues. Supporting/caring people will ask about you and your family. They have a comfortable look about them, with comfortable clothes, an open posture, and a kind, gentle facial expression. Their offices have touches of home, with family photographs, plants, and a comfortable seating arrangement. Supporting/caring people need personal recognition and evidence that you care about them (not just their work).

Directing/Guiding

These people value results, accomplishments, action, and loyalty. They are not comfortable with self-disclosure, and will rarely reveal anything about themselves other than their achievements and activities. They are not particularly interested in hearing about you, your family, or your problems. They prefer to keep things impersonal. Directing/guiding people have a serious, almost stern, look about them, with closed postures and a military bearing. Their offices reflect a serious, organized place where things get done, and there are few personal touches other than symbols of their accomplishments or their beliefs and values. The seating arrangement is formal and distancing.

Analytical

These people value information, accuracy, logical thinking, and organization. They have a great need for structure and schedules and tend to be perfectionists. Like directing/guiding people, they prefer to keep things impersonal and will not reveal much about themselves, except to share ideas. They reveal the least amount of emotion of any of the personality types and have an almost expressionless look about them most of the time. Analytical people may be obsessively neat and organized; or they may have so much information in their offices—data, manuals, reports, and so on—that there are stacks everywhere. They do have a system for what appears to be clutter, and they can find what they need. If they have seating for guests in their offices, it may be covered with piles of information.

Expressive

These people value excitement, stimulation, fun, spontaneity, and attention. They are the most animated and openly emotional of the four types of people. They are self-disclosing and talk about themselves a lot. They draw attention to themselves with bright colors, flamboyant dress or behavior, or with their creativity and humor. Expressive people have toys in their offices, color, art, music, and (if they can get away with it) unusual seating arrangements and personal touches. They display a wide range of facial expressions and react quickly and often dramatically to what others say and do.

Remember: All four types of people are okay! They each have their own communication style, values, strengths, and weaknesses, and they each have the potential to be consistently assertive in their own way. People tend to think of their own type as the best and view the others as inferior, but that kind of thinking is not consistent with the assertive philosophy you are learning to follow. Learn to recognize each type so you can effectively communicate with them and put self-fulfilling prophecy to work by concentrating on their positive characteristics.

As you practice matching the style of each type of person, you will develop your own underlying strengths. You will find that matching styles becomes easier, and you will become aware of new abilities, perceptions, and characteristics emerging in yourself. What a nice bonus from learning to communicate more effectively with others!

Assertive Power
Steps

Four Steps to Assertive Communication

Even if you successfully choose assertive words, correctly assess the other person's personality type and the style of assertiveness to which they might best respond, and deliver your words with the appropriate body language, there is no guarantee that the other person will respond with the desired cooperative response! You never have more than 50% of the control in any human interaction, and the other person may ignore your skillful assertiveness.

This is when you need to be prepared to increase the power of your assertiveness. You continue to be assertive, but you become a little more insistent, a little more emotional, or a little more commanding to ensure that you get what you want in the situation. Think of it as "power steps"—you start at the bottom step, which is basic assertive behavior; and if that does not work, you take one step up in power. If that does not work, you take another step, and another, if needed. At no point do you have to resort to aggressive behavior.

Step 1: Repeat the Question or Statement

One way to add power to your assertiveness is to repeat your first communication. Some have referred to this as the *broken record*. You ask the same question or make the same statement. Make sure that you have good eye contact and that you speak with confident, assertive voice tones. You may want to emphasize certain words the second time to increase the chances of getting your point across.

Assertive statements: *"Will you please tell me how to find Mr. Green's office?" (No response from the other person)*

"Will you please tell me how to find Mr. Green's office?"

Step 2: Command, Don't Ask

If the other person continues to ignore you or refuses to cooperate, switch from asking to commanding. To most people, a directive sounds more powerful than a request. Therefore, learn to use the *request* for the majority of people (the most notable exception being the directing/guiding type of person). The average person will hear your request as polite and appropriate, there is less risk of sounding pushy, and you can change to a *command* if the request does not produce results.

Assertive statement: *"Please give me directions to Mr. Green's office."*

Before considering other ways to increase the power of your assertiveness, practice escalating your assertiveness just a little when your first effort is not successful.

Situation: Commanding

You are participating in a staff meeting and want to make a point about the topic being discussed. Assume a topic and write your assertive statement below:

_____

_____

Alas, no one responds. Perhaps they have not heard you, or they may be choosing to ignore you. If you choose to repeat the original statement, write below which words you would emphasize to add a small amount of power.

_____

_____

Still no one responds! Write below what you would say to be even more emphatic about your point, without becoming aggressive.

_____

_____

Now ask someone to evaluate your practice efforts to verify that you have been assertive each time.

Step 3: Add Emotion

If your efforts are still unsuccessful, you can express your emotions as another way to add power to your assertiveness. People are unaccustomed to others expressing emotions openly and honestly, and by doing so you add considerable power to your communication.

Assertive statements: *"I suggest that we bring in a consultant to help us with this." (No response from the others)*

"I suggest that we bring in a consultant to help us with this." (Still no response)

"Please tell me what you think of my suggestion to bring in a consultant to help us." (No response or a dismissive response)

"Now I'm getting angry! Please give me a serious response to my suggestion."

You will probably get some attention with the last one! This level of assertiveness would be inappropriate earlier in the process, but after three attempts to be heard, it is quite appropriate. Not only will it result in respectful attention, it will likely produce apologies from the others. You do not have to apologize for expressing your emotions, and it is recommended that you do not. You are completely within your rights to respond emotionally if you do not receive respectful responses from others when you are making a serious effort to communicate assertively. Apologies diminish your power. If you do receive the response you desire, it is a good idea to express appreciation.

Situation: Adding Emotion

Assume that you are asking someone to assist you with a task or project, or that you are asking for another person's ideas or preferences. Write your request below.

_____

_____

Assume that you get no response or an insincere one. Write a command version below.

_____

_____

Assume that this second effort receives no better response. Write an assertive communication in which you express your feelings about the situation.

_____

_____

Now ask someone to evaluate your practice efforts to be sure that you have been assertive each time.

You may be tempted by now to become aggressive in order to get your needs met, but please do not yield to this temptation. By remaining assertive, you have a better chance of getting cooperation without the risk of retaliation. When you use aggression to get your way, you must be prepared to receive aggression in return from the person whose rights you violated!

Step 4: Introduce Consequences

A final way to add power to your assertiveness is to introduce consequences. Consequences are not threats, because they are not harmful or inappropriate. They are simply statements of what you intend to do if you do not get the cooperation or results you desire. Following are some criteria for successful consequences.

➤ Consequences need to be stated in advance. The other person deserves an opportunity to change his or her behavior to prevent the consequence. Taking an action without prior notice could be interpreted as inappropriate and aggressive.

➤ Consequences need to be strong but believable. The action needs to be something undesirable, but if it is too extreme, the other person will not believe that you will actually do it. Empty threats are ignored.

➤ You must be prepared to follow through and implement the consequence if necessary. If the other person decides to test you and you do not take the action you said you would, you lose credibility and power for dealing with this person in the future. He or she may also tell others, and you will lose credibility with them, too.

Some Examples

After several attempts to get someone to stop taking things from your desk without permission:

> *"If you take anything else from my desk without asking first, I will inform the department manager and the security office about this repeated pattern."*

After you have asked one of your car pool drivers to stay within the speed limit and stop following cars too closely:

> *"Pat, I really am uncomfortable with your driving so fast and following other cars so closely. If you continue to do this, I will drop out of the car pool."*

Situation: Introducing Consequences

Assume that you have purchased an expensive new suit. The purchase price included alterations. You were in a hurry and did not try on the suit. When you put it on the next day, you discovered that the sleeves were a little too long, there were a couple of wrinkles across the shoulders, and the waist was a little loose. You have decided to return the suit for additional alteration and expect this additional tailoring to be free. How will you word your original request?

_____

_____

Assume that you are told that additional alterations will cost another $35. What will you say to get the store representative to provide the alterations at no charge?

_____

_____

Assume that this effort fails. The salesperson informs you that the store's policy requires that additional alterations made after the customer has accepted the clothing must be paid for, and he (or she) does not have the authority to break this rule. What will you say?

_____

_____

Assume that this third attempt is not successful. Write a statement of consequences in the space below.

_____

_____

Compare your statements with the Author's in the Appendix.

Assertive

Confrontation

70

Defining the Problem

Perhaps the most challenging time to be assertive is when another person's behavior is unacceptable to you and you need to talk with this person about changing the behavior. What do you think of when you hear the word *confrontation*? Do you envision yelling and screaming? Do you imagine anger, tears, blame and accusation, denials and hurt feelings? Most people have only unpleasant experiences involving confrontation, and have no idea how confrontation can be handled assertively, even caringly.

One important aspect of handling confrontation assertively is defining the problem in such a way that you can talk with the other person about the problem without communicating disapproval or disrespect. This requires that you learn to define the specific behavior that you find unacceptable, rather than seeing the other person as unacceptable. This may take some practice!

WHAT'S THE PROBLEM?

For each of the following examples, fill in the "label" that someone might use to describe the person or the person's attitude or motivation. This is what most people do—label the other person—and this labeling is one of the reasons why a confrontation attempt may fail. After identifying the label that seems to fit the person, write a description of the specific behavior without using any judgmental words or personal adjectives.

Terry, a teenager, takes a seat at the dinner table, looks at the meal placed there, rolls his eyes toward the ceiling, and says, "I can't believe we're having this again! Don't you have any imagination? This is the most boring food in town!"

What label describes Terry? _____

What is the specific behavior? _____

_____

Rosa arrives for the 8:00 A.M. staff meeting at about 8:15 A.M. and, while avoiding eye contact with the others, finds an empty chair. While she is arranging several folders of materials and searching through her purse for something else, she knocks over her coffee cup. She grabs for the folders to save them from the coffee, and the contents of the folders fly everywhere. Rosa utters an expletive, collapses into her chair, and buries her face in her hands.

What label describes Rosa? _____

What is the specific behavior? _____

_____

The labels are easier than the behavior descriptions, aren't they? Most of us have been judging and labeling others since we were children, so learning to factually describe specific behavior does take practice.

Compare your responses to the Authors' suggestions in the Appendix.

Five Tools for Successful Confrontation

To resolve situations such as these, the confronter needs to inform the other person about the behavior, and the results of that behavior, in such a way that the person feels respected and will be more likely to respond cooperatively. The following tools will help you learn to confront behaviors in just this manner.

1. Identify which assertive style will work best.

Which type of personality will you be addressing? The confrontation will be more successful if you use the other person's natural style. The analytical style is recommended for both the analytical and the directing/guiding types of people. A directive approach is a little strong for confrontational situations.

2. Define the specific behavior to be confronted.

Identify what the other person does that you wish he or she did not do, or what the person does not do that you wish he or she did. Define what the person does differently from the way you would prefer. Avoid using judgmental or accusatory words. Be factual.

Example: Factual descriptions of the behaviors from the two preceding examples: making disparaging remarks and arriving after the starting time.

Practice: Use a current or recent problem situation in your own life that involves another person and describe the behavior of this person.

_____

_____

3. Describe the results of the behavior.

What undesirable impact does the behavior have on you? Does it cost you time, money, effort? Does the behavior affect productivity, customer service, quality, or morale? It is important to identify how the behavior contributes to a problem so you can explain to the other person why you want him or her to change. These are the logical, rational reasons for changing that enable the other person to consider altering his or her behavior without feeling attacked or judged.

Example: Terry's behavior creates stress for other family members, which may affect their health. It also sets an example that younger children may follow and invites bad feelings, rather than an open discussion of alternatives. Rosa's behavior disrupts discussion and sets an example.

Practice: Using the same problem described in Step 2, identify two or three possible results of the person's behavior.

_____

_____

4. Identify your own feelings.

When the behavior of others creates a problem for you, it is natural to have some feelings about the situation. These emotions will most likely be negative, rather than positive, and it is important for you to be aware of them, to acknowledge them, and to express them. Denying feelings and holding them in only creates problems. You can do this so much that you experience physical symptoms such as sleeplessness, headaches, or worse. When you do finally let out these pent-up feelings, you may do so inappropriately and regret what you say and do.

Telling someone how you feel actually adds power to your confrontation. Remember the lessons from Part 3 about how to identify your feelings and how to express them with "I" statements.

Example: Concerned that our family will not enjoy dinner together, disappointed and annoyed about the late arrivals.

Practice: Using the same real problem you used in Step 2, identify your feelings toward the other person and about the results of the behavior or other aspects of the situation, and write them as "I" statements.

_____

_____

5.   Define the goal you hope to accomplish.

It is not enough to confront someone about his or her behavior; you must get a commitment from the person to change. Without this commitment, you have accomplished little beyond getting something "off your chest" (which is okay, but not enough to resolve the problem). What do you want? Do you want the other person to stop the behavior in question? Do you want the person to do something other than what he or she has been doing? Do you want some ideas from him or her about how to resolve the problem? This last approach is strongly recommended, because people are most likely to follow through with a change that was their own idea!

A final suggestion for this element of the confrontation is to ask for what you want. As stated earlier, a command is a little strong for most people in a confrontation.

Example: *"Will you please give me some suggestions for meals, Terry? Are you willing to be responsible for preparing dinner one evening each week? I would appreciate your help."*

Practice: Decide what you want in your problem situation and write your request below.

_____

_____

Taking time to think through the situation and identify these five tools will help you respond more assertively. Responding spontaneously might result in your being nonassertive or aggressive. With practice, you can learn to handle such situations spontaneously and be successfully assertive. Most people will need to plan and rehearse several confrontations as they learn to think and act assertively.

When you put all the pieces together, how does an assertive confrontation sound? Remember that this will be a dialogue, not a lecture. You begin the discussion by saying something about the situation, and then the other person responds. What you say next is determined by the person's response and what you plan to accomplish. The better prepared you are, the more flexible you can be when you get unexpected responses from the other person.

A Confrontation with Terry

Assuming that Terry is an Expressive teenager, a confrontative dialogue might sound like the following:

Parent: *"Wow, Terry! You really don't like the menu in this joint, huh?"*

Terry: *"That's right! It's boring. We always have the same stuff!"*

Parent: *"Terry, I'm concerned that your expressing yourself with such disapproving behavior and words will affect our being able to enjoy this time together as a family. If you would like more variety in the meal planning, are you willing to help me by making some suggestions for meals or even being responsible for one meal a week?"*

Terry: *"No way! I don't have time for that."*

Parent: *"Okay. Will you agree not to make such negative remarks at the table in the future?"*

A Confrontation with Rosa

Assuming that Rosa is a Supporting/Caring person, a confrontation might begin as follows:

Manager: *"Rosa, you seemed really flustered in the meeting this morning and uncomfortable with the disruption you caused."*

Rosa: *"Oh, yes, I was so embarrassed when I spilled my coffee! I knew I was interrupting by coming late again, and I was trying not to call attention to myself, and then I did that stupid thing!"*

Manager: *"We all have our bad days, Rosa. I was disappointed when you arrived at 8:15 because you promised me you would be on time when you were late last week. What can you do to make sure that you will be on time for our future meetings?"*

Do you see how the confrontation is tailored to match the other person's style? Did you notice that not all of the tools were used in each situation? Nevertheless, thinking about all five tools helps prepare you to go in whatever direction the other person seems willing to go. Matching the person's style helps to create a better rapport and increases the probability of getting a cooperative response.

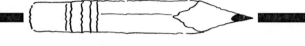

CONFRONTATION DIALOGUE EXERCISE

Use the real problem situation that you have thought through and practice writing what you will say. Guess how the other person would respond and decide what you would say after that response to continue negotiating for what you want.

Your opening statement: _____

_____

The other's response: _____

_____

Your next statement: _____

_____

The next big step for you will be to actually talk with this person in an effort to resolve the problem. This may take some courage and you may not be completely successful, but you will have taken an important step along the road to becoming more assertive. Even if you do not resolve the problem, you will increase your self-respect, and will probably earn a little respect from the other person as well.

Active Listening

You may be concerned about what to do if the other person responds emotionally and defensively to your confrontation. That is a legitimate concern and a likely occurrence! Probably the most effective technique for handling such responses is empathic listening, or active listening.*

The idea is to listen carefully when the other person responds to what you have said, and prove that you heard and understood by restating what you heard. Your restatement needs to be paraphrased so you won't sound like an echo. Try the following effective formula:

Paraphrase content. Summarize the information or thoughts that the other person expressed to you. This establishes that you understood what he or she said.

Acknowledge feelings. Even though the speaker may not have said what he or she is feeling, trust your intuition, make a guess, and put the speaker's feelings into words. This demonstrates your empathy.

End with a "check-out" question. Signal that you have finished responding by asking a question such as "Right?"; "Is that what you said?"; "Did I hear you correctly?"; or something similar. He or she will either confirm or correct you, and will feel heard and understood, which helps someone be less defensive and emotional.

EFFECTIVE LISTENING

EFFECTIVE RESPONSE

*For a complete treatment of this technique, read Self-Empowerment *by Sam Lloyd and Tina Berthelot, Crisp Series.*

Developing Positive Assertiveness

RESTATING WHAT YOU HEAR

Terry might react to being confronted about his dinnertime behavior by saying, "Get real, Mom (or Dad)! All you ever talk about is quality time. We don't have any quality time in this family anymore!"

What is Terry's unstated emotion? _____

_____

What is the content of the message? _____

_____

What would be your restatement? _____

_____

Rosa might respond to being confronted about her late arrival by saying, "I'm sorry. I'm just overwhelmed with everything that's going on in my life right now. I can't seem to get caught up because things keep going wrong, and I'm getting farther and farther behind!"

What is Rosa feeling? _____

_____

What is the content of the message? _____

_____

What would be your restatement? _____

_____

Compare your responses to those in the Appendix.

CASE STUDY: LISTEN TO HIM

A participant in a company training program was taught the technique of restating content and acknowledging feelings, and she was asked to practice with someone before the second day of the program. The young woman decided to practice with her roommate, who was soon to be her husband. She described her experience in class the next morning as an eye-opening experience! When they both were home at the end of their workday, she used her new listening approach without telling him what she was doing. He said, "Boy, I had a really rough day. My boss was on a rampage!" She responded, "Sounds like you're glad this day's over because things were pretty tough at work, huh?"

At this point in her classroom narrative, she stopped to explain that her fiancé was a restless type of fellow who would usually walk around when they talked, sometimes walking into another room during their conversations. She described him as "antsy." As she continued reporting her experience, she said, "When I restated what he had said, he just stopped, turned around, pulled up a chair next to where I was sitting, and we had a real conversation!" After the training class stopped laughing, she said that they talked for almost an hour and he remained seated the entire time. She was delighted and amazed that her listening responses had produced such a dramatic result.

AUTHOR'S RESPONSE

It is often the case that we have the greatest difficulty with communication in our most significant relationships. Few people have any training in managing relationships, and resolving problems in our important relationships can be challenging. But learning how to resolve difficulties in a win-win manner can make a marvelous difference in any relationship. Like everything else in this book, however, it does take practice. We were not taught these techniques and skills when we were young, and none of us will change lifetime patterns of behavior overnight!

The following worksheet may assist you with improving your skills in this area. You can use this worksheet for planning and sharing with your significant others, and as a script for your problem-solving discussions.

TALKING OUT PROBLEMS

1. **Set the stage**. Say something such as, "I value our relationship and I appreciate your willingness to help resolve problems when they come up."

2. **State the problem**. "I am_____(concerned, angry, and so on) about a problem and I want your help with it. To me, the problem seems to be

   _____ ."

   (As much as possible, avoid using "you" statements when stating the problem.)

3. **Own your part**. "My part in the problem is that I _____

   _____ ."

   (State what you do or do not do, what you assume, how you react, and so on)

4. **Ask for the other side**. "How do you see it?" "What do you think about it?" "How do you feel about it?"

5. **Listen and restate**.

6. **Make your offer**. "To help solve the problem (improve the situation) I am willing to _____ ."

7. **Ask for what you want**. "Will you please_____

   _____ ?"

8. **Negotiate agreement on a contract**. Summarize what each person will give or do.

9. **Set a time for evaluation**. Agree upon a date to evaluate how your solution has worked.

10. **Discuss how you have done**. If you have done well, have a celebration! Discuss how you can improve, negotiate a new agreement, express appreciation for each other, and renew your commitment to the relationship. If you have not done well, discuss how you can improve or how you might approach the problem differently.

Goals for the Present and Future

To avoid taking wrong turns and slipping into former patterns of nonassertive and/or aggressive behavior, practice assertive behavior regularly. First take short trips, and then longer journeys.

Short Trips (Short-term goals):

Once a day during the next week, spend 10 to 15 minutes at the end of each working day writing assertive statements about situations involving you or observed by you. Use nonassertive and aggressive incidents and write down how they could have been handled assertively.

Each evening before turning out the light, read the psychological "reprogramming" cards you completed on page 21, after achieving a state of relaxation. Do this for three weeks.

At least once each week for the next three weeks, initiate a conversation with someone whose natural style is different from your own. Practice using this style. Notice the positive features of this style and try using them yourself.

Short-Term Goals

By now you probably have some goals you want to accomplish. Write your short-term goals in the spaces below. Remember to make them achievable and positive.

During the next three weeks I will:

1.

2.

3.

Longer Journeys (Long-term goals):

Enroll and participate in an assertive training course or seminar.

Identify a situation or activity that you did not handle assertively in the past and plan how to handle it assertively in the future. Write out what you will say. Practice your delivery with a friend and then do it!

Make additional "reprogramming" cards and use them. Review your old cards on a regular basis.

Read books about assertiveness, personal growth, or communication skills within the next month. Cassette tapes and computer-based training programs may also be helpful.

Long-Term Goals

Write down the long-term goals you want to achieve.

During the next three months I will:

1.

2.

3.

Some of the goals you may want to accomplish might require more than three months. If so, write those goals in the spaces below.

Within the next year I will:

1.

2.

3.

Giving Yourself Credit for Success

Reliving a special trip through snapshots or movies can be fun, rekindling feelings of pleasure you experienced originally. Following are some suggestions to help you reinforce the success of your new assertiveness skills.

Tell a friend or family member about a successful assertive experience you had. Ask this person to comment on your success.

➤ Keep a journal. Write down your assertive successes. The entry does not have to be anything unusual, difficult, or dramatic—just an example of assertive behavior. Review your journal regularly. Reading about past successes can provide a real shot of positive energy whenever you are feeling low.

➤ Immediately after you have been assertive and are pleased with the outcome, take a few minutes to mentally record the experience. Close your eyes and see the scene as vividly as possible—feel your power, confidence, and satisfaction; and hear your words and voice. While re-experiencing the success with your senses, select a gesture to "set" the experience (for example, squeeze a thumbnail, pull an earlobe, and so on). In the future, whenever you want to recall the scene and return to assertiveness, repeat the gesture.

➤ Reread this book next week and then again in three months. Redo the exercises. Compare the results to your earlier work. Define some new short-term and long-term goals. The assertive road to interpersonal effectiveness never ends.

➤ Share with others. Tell them what you learned about yourself (use "I" language!). Share your goals. This increases your commitment to them. Give copies of this book to others and share with them after they have completed it.

A P P E N D I X

Summary and Review

Following is a quick review of what has been presented in this book. There are three fundamental behaviors: nonassertive, assertive, and aggressive. Of these styles, assertive behavior is the most desirable.

First you took a reading of your own assertiveness. Next you learned to identify each behavior style, and you learned about the basic personality groups: thinkers, feelers, and doers. These initial insights were provided to help you move toward a "win-win" philosophy of assertiveness.

The five Ps of successful change were then presented: protection, potency, permission, practice, and proof. Rereading that section will ensure that you do what is required to develop and achieve your assertiveness. Remember that self-fulfilling prophecy is a real phenomenon and follow an assertive philosophy. If you expect to be assertive, you will create more success in your life and influence others in a positive way.

Next you learned about the power of psychological programming and how to use it as a positive tool. You also learned that being assertive requires us to accept responsibility for our thoughts, feelings, and behaviors; and to use direct, honest, respectful words and accompanying body language.

A refinement of your communication skills was then covered, which encouraged the development of your ability to use the four assertive styles: supporting/caring, directing/guiding, analytical, and expressive. You had an opportunity to identify and practice each style.

After you learned the basics of being assertive and matching assertive styles, you learned several techniques for adding power to your assertiveness: being patient and repeating, emphasizing words and phrases, switching from a request to a command, expressing emotions, and stating consequences to improve your odds of getting what you want.

The challenge of confronting others was treated with a five-part formula for preparing what you will say to open a negotiation with someone about changing a behavior that you find unacceptable. You practiced identifying each of these important elements as you thought through a real problem situation. A worksheet/script was provided to assist you with talking through a problem with someone.

You were given an opportunity to define some short-term and long-term goals, and to practice creating assertive responses for given situations. Finally, you were encouraged to continue down the assertive road to interpersonal effectiveness. This book has given you the tools you need to become assertive—it is up to you to apply what you have learned.

Remember: Practice will not make you perfect, but it will help you become more assertive. Please read this book again in a week or two, practice your new techniques and skills, and enjoy the rewards of being an assertive person!

Author's Answers

Behavior Styles Quiz, Page 4

1. **AG**–Accusatory, exaggerated, blameful; invites defensiveness.

2. **NAS**–Hesitant, passive, apologetic, invites disregard.

3. **NAS**–Plans are only plans and can be changed. This is a subtle form of dishonesty and one of the most common ways of avoiding having to say no.

4. **AS**–Honest and respectful; invites cooperation.

5. **AS**–Honest, tactful, and firm but appreciative (compare to #3).

6. **AG**–Sarcastic and blameful; invites defensiveness.

7. **NAS**–Self-deprecating and defensive; invites disrespect.

8. **NAS**–Hesitant and deferential; possibly dishonest about wants.

9. **AS**–Enthusiastic, genuine, and cooperative.

10. **AS**–Direct and respective; invites cooperation.

A Personality Quiz, Page 6

If you answered statements 1, 4, 7, 11, and 12 as true and the others false, you are an active initiator who prefers one-on-one interaction. You are a thinker who plans, and you are careful and methodical.

If you answered statements 2, 6, 9, 10, 11, and 13 as true and most others false, you are an active initiator who is sociable and caring. You are a feeler in touch with your emotions, and you value personal relationships and want to please people.

If you answered statements 5, 8, 10, and 14 true and most others false, you are more passive than initiative with people. You are less involved with people and more interested in physical activities. You are a doer who enjoys the pleasure of being active. You are not likely to be comfortable around others when they discuss feelings.

What about statement 3? People who like to eat lunch alone need solitude. Thinkers and some doers often are more withdrawing and involving. This means they are comfortable being alone. Most feelers, many thinkers, and some doers have a greater need to be with people.

Of course, there are many other psychological groupings and sophisticated questionnaires that identify these groups. In this book, we have tried to keep things simple, and limited ourselves to three general groupings: thinkers, feelers, and doers. These three are sufficient to provide insight into some of the most basic automatic behaviors and orientations toward life. Awareness of which group you are in should help you understand why you are more comfortable in certain situations than others. It also helps explain why others often approach life differently than you do.

Each personality type is okay! It is natural to consider the group we identify with as somehow "better" than the others. One type, however, is not better than another; it is simply different. All types are essential, and all make a contribution to life, organizations, and families. Each has different strengths, and each approaches work and life differently. Accepting this reality is an important step toward developing an assertive, win-win approach with others.

Nonassertive, Assertive, or Aggressive, Page 44

1. **Aggressive**. This posture makes a person look larger, much like birds fluff feathers, mammals raise neck hairs, and some fish and reptiles inflate themselves.

2. **Assertive**. This may be a comforting gesture or a way to communicate emphasis.

3. **Aggressive**. This entraps the other person and is a controlling maneuver, rather than an affectionate or comforting one.

4. **Nonassertive**. The shifting movement communicates anxiety.

5. **Nonassertive**. Head bobbing usually signals, "I want to please you." Occasional nods may communicate attentiveness.

6. **Aggressive**. Most people perceive this as a power display.

7. **Nonassertive**. Looking down frequently or steadily communicates anxiety.

8. **Assertive**. This probably signals interest and attentiveness.

9. **Aggressive**. When the tapping communicates impatience or boredom—it might come across as nervousness (accompanying signals makes the difference).

10. **Assertive**. This looks relaxed and attentive.

11. **Aggressive**. This is the most frequent interpretation. Others include "closed mind," impatient, bored, uncaring, and defensive.

12. **Nonassertive**. This posture usually signals deference and it is almost impossible to retain for any length of time. It could appear relaxed with a peer.

13. **Aggressive**. This signal usually looks disapproving or threatening.

14. **Nonassertive**. Twirling the pencil probably communicates anxiety. Doing it while listening to someone could signal impatience.

15. **Aggressive**. This is another subtle power display.

These answers represent the most common interpretation of the signals.

Which Style Is Which, Page 52

1. **A**   A straightforward statement of facts

2. **E**   Spontaneous enthusiasm

3. **S/C**   A personal acknowledgment with gratitude

4. **D/G**   A statement of opinion and a concern for results

5. **D/G**   Commanding someone to provide information

6. **S/C**   Recognizing anothers interests, and indicating support while preventing a diversion

7. **A**   Providing information about timing, and indicating support while preventing a diversion

8. **E**   Action words, stating a dislike, and enthusiasm for the suggested new topic

9. **S/C**   Acknowledging enthusiasm and expressing appreciation for cooperation

10. **A**   Informative, factual, unemotional

Can You Identify These People, Page 57

The aisle passenger correctly assessed the middle-seat passenger as a doer who did not respond to the analytical style, which provided information about which style would be successful. Many doers use a directing/guiding style and exhibit pride in what they have achieved with visible signs of success. Using a directive aimed at "doing" established rapport instantly. The analytical communicator had no success involving the middle-seat passenger in conversation because the choice of words used was inappropriate for the directing/guiding communicator.

1. Analytical

2. Directing/Guiding

3. Doer

Situation: Introducing Consequences, Page 68

"When I put on my new suit I discovered several things about the fit that are not quite satisfactory, and I have brought it back so you can fix them. Will you please take care of it for me?"

"My understanding was that alterations were included in the price and that a good fit was guaranteed, so I will appreciate your making these few small adjustments without charge."

"When I picked up the suit I explained that I did not have time to try it on, and I was informed that would be no problem. If I had tried it on then, I would not have accepted the suit as it is. If you cannot authorize additional alterations without charge, please get someone who can."

"If you will not get your supervisor to authorize this and if you insist on charging me for additional alterations, I will not shop here in the future. I will inform the Better Business Bureau about the incident, and I will also inform the Consumer Hotline program of Channel 8 television."

Remember that the whole idea of being assertive is to create win-win outcomes. By being patient and persistent with people, while adding small increments of power to your communication efforts, you have a better chance of getting what you want while allowing the other person to feel respected. Their respect for you will grow as well, which will make future negotiations with this person even easier. Most people prefer dealing with others who know how to be powerful without being intimidating, rude, or manipulative.

With practice, your skills for adding power will improve, and your confidence and self-esteem* will grow. As your confidence and self-esteem develop, being assertive becomes even easier.

---

*To help you develop self-esteem, read Developing Self-Esteem by Connie Palladino, Crisp Series.

What's the Problem, Page 72

Terry could be described as insolent, sullen, disrespectful or insubordinate, among other things. The specific behavior is making disparaging remarks about the meal.

Rosa could be described as tardy, disorganized, clumsy, or uncommunicative. The specific behavior is arriving at 8:15 a.m. for an 8:00 a.m. meeting, spilling coffee, and dropping papers while attempting to save them from the coffee.

In each of these cases, it would be appropriate for the others involved to confront the behavior. The challenge is to confront the specific behavior, rather than the person. If people feel they are being attacked, they will respond defensively and refuse to cooperate. If they hear that they are being judged, they will respond defensively and probably judge in return.

Restating What You Hear, Page 80

Terry seems to be feeling disappointed, hurt, angry, and frustrated.

Terry's message was that the family is lacking in quality time together.

An active listening response might be as follows: "Terry, you sound frustrated and disappointed about our not having much time together. Is that right?"

Rosa seems to be feeling overwhelmed, helpless, frustrated, and despondent. The content of her message is that she has experienced a number of problems and is having difficulty keeping up with her responsibilities.

An active listening response might be as follows: "Rosa, you seem really frustrated about a lot of problems in your life and not being able to keep up with your work. Right?"

Although this may sound simplistic to you, the person with whom you are communicating will very likely feel your empathy and understanding, and will not even be aware that you have just restated what you heard him or her say. The emotional impact of this type of listening response is powerful and positive, and the result is usually a reduction of stress and defensiveness.

One empathetic response will not result in a person becoming calm and rational if he or she responded powerfully to your confrontation. You may need to listen and restate several times before the person returns to a normal level of emotion and a willingness to hear you continue your negotiation. It does work, but you need to practice a lot to become skillful.

Follow-Up Practice Exercises

Follow-up practice is an important requirement for changing old behavior patterns. The examples and challenges in this section will facilitate your practice. Rather than doing all of these at once, it will probably be more helpful for you to do a few and then wait several days before doing more. This will help you keep thinking about what you have learned and encourage you to remember and review what you have read when you come back to complete more of the follow-up practice exercises.

Practice 1

Workplace Situations:

A co-worker has promised to provide you with important information by a certain date and time, but does not deliver. This is the second time this person has failed to keep a commitment to you. What will you say to communicate your thoughts/feelings/needs?

_____

_____

The co-worker responds to your words by saying, "I'm only human, you know! I can't always control what others demand from me, particularly my boss! I did my best, but I just couldn't get everything done in time!" Using the active listening feedback technique, how will you respond to the co-worker?

_____

_____

Home Situation:

A telephone call interrupts your dinner. It is someone calling from a charitable organization that you support to request an additional donation. You dislike having your meal interrupted by solicitations and you want the organization to stop calling. What do you say?

_____

_____

Social Situation:

At a gathering in a friend's home, a guest is telling you with loud and exaggerated words that your opinion on the gun control issue is wrong and that only an uninformed idiot could support your position! What do you say?

_____

_____

There are many possible ways to handle each of these situations assertively, and your responses may be right on target. To test your new skills in developing positive assertiveness, compare your responses to the author's suggestions on the next page. Another option is to ask someone else to read your responses and tell you how the words sound to them. This will be particularly helpful if the other person has also read this book and knows what assertiveness is all about!

The Author's suggested responses appear on the next page.

Practice 1: Author's Suggested Responses

Work Situation: "I am really disappointed that you don't have the information for me. I thought we had a clear understanding that you would have it ready by today at this time. How soon will you have it for me?"

An active listening response to the co-worker: "So you're saying that since making the commitment to me you have had other demands put on you and are pretty stressed trying to get everything done on time. Right?"

Home Situation: "I do support your organization with donations, but I do not like being called at home in the evening. Please remove my name from your calling list."

Social Situation: "I suggest we just agree to disagree and stop this discussion before either of us says something even more inappropriate than what has already been said. Okay?"

Practice 2

Workplace Situation:

An important customer has just asked you for a discount larger than you are authorized to approve. You also know that your boss will not agree to such a large price reduction either. What will you say to this important customer?

_____

_____

Home Situation:

Your significant other has purchased a very expensive item for your home without consulting with you. The store has a "no refund" policy. Although you like the item, you are disturbed about your significant other spending such a large amount of money on an item that cannot be returned without even considering your preferences. What will you say?

_____

_____

Social Situation:

Your neighbor has borrowed an expensive tool (lawnmower or drill, for example) and somehow managed to break it. It seems to be broken beyond repair, and your neighbor has apologized profusely but has not offered to replace it. You believe that the neighbor should pay to replace your tool. What will you say?

_____

_____

Again, ask someone to evaluate your responses to find out how another person responds to what you chose to say. Remember that what you said may be assertive and the other person may feel uncomfortable with your response because of their own issues.

The Author's suggested responses appear on the next page.

Practice 2: Author's Suggested Responses

Work Situation: " <Customer's name>, we value your business a lot and want to give you the best price we can. I can authorize an additional discount of 5%, and I will have accounts receivable make that discount retroactive to your last order as well as apply it to your future orders."

Home Situation: " <Significant other's name>, I do like what you bought. I'm surprised and disappointed that you bought it without giving me the opportunity to participate in the decision. I would like for us to work out an agreement about future purchases for anything that costs more than a couple of hundred dollars. Does that sound reasonable?"

Social Situation: " <Neighbor's name>, I know you feel bad about breaking my tool and this is an uncomfortable situation for both of us. It was an expensive, high-quality tool, and I will appreciate your replacing it with another just like it. Okay?"

Practice 3

Congratulations for continuing to practice your assertiveness skills with these follow-up examples. Following are a few more, and I hope they are getting easier for you!

Work Situation:

Your boss is giving you some feedback about your performance. The feedback has been fairly positive, but you have received practically no specifics about what you have done well and you want to learn more about what your boss likes about your work. How will you ask for what you want?

_____

_____

Home Situation:

Your parents have called to let you know that they are planning to come for a visit of two weeks. You and your significant other agree that such a long visit would be stressful for both of you and that you would be more comfortable with a visit of five or six days. What will you say to communicate your preferences?

_____

_____

Social Situation:

A neighbor down the block owns a large dog. The dog is allowed to roam the neighborhood and has chosen your yard as the ideal place to "do his business." You dislike having dog waste in your yard, and plan to speak with the dog's owner about the situation. What will you say?

_____

_____

The Author's suggested responses appear on the following page.
You may also find it helpful to ask those who know you well their
opinion of your own responses.

Practice 3: Author's Suggested Responses

Work Situation: "I'm glad that you like my work, <boss's name>. To help me continue to do what you want in the way you like, will you please give me some examples of what you have seen?"

Home Situation: "We are happy to have you come for a visit, Mom and Dad. We would prefer to keep the visit to about five or six days so we can spend a lot of time with you. Longer visits create a problem for us with our work schedules and other commitments. Will that work for you?"

Social Situation: "<Neighbor's name>, I know you like to let your dog run and get his exercise, and you may not even be aware that he frequently does his business in my yard when he is out. I don't like seeing the result and I sure don't like smelling it when the weather gets warm. Will you please pick up after him?"

Keep practicing with everyday situations and you will find that being assertive becomes increasingly natural for you. Please remember that you will still choose to be nonassertive and aggressive at times, and that just proves you are human! The more often you are assertive, the more you will find that your relationships improve, your stress level is reduced, and your wants and needs are satisfied more consistently.

Additional Reading

Bellman, Geoffrey. *Getting Things Done When You Are Not In Charge.* NY: Fireside, 1993.

Bradford, David & Allan Cohen. *Influence Without Authority.* NY: John Wiley & Sons, 1990.

Burley-Allen, Madelyn. *Managing Assertively.* NY: John Wiley & Sons, 1981.

Clarke, Jean. *Who, Me Lead A Group?* Seattle, WA: Parenting Press, 1998.

Fisher, Roger & W. Ury. *Getting To Yes.* Boston, MA: Houghton Mifflin, 1981.

LaBorde, Genie Z. *Influencing With Integrity.* Syntony, 1983.

Lloyd, Sam & Tina Berthelot. *Self-Empowerment, Revised Edition.* Crisp Series, 2003.

Lloyd, Sam. *Leading Teams: The Skills for Success.* American Media, 1996.

NOTES

NOTES

Also Available

Books•Videos•Computer-Based Training Products

If you enjoyed this book, we have great news for you. There are over 200 books available in the *Crisp Fifty-Minute™ Series*. For more information visit us online at www.axzopress.com

Subject Areas Include:

Management
Human Resources
Communication Skills
Personal Development
Sales/Marketing
Finance
Coaching and Mentoring
Customer Service/Quality
Small Business and Entrepreneurship
Training
Life Planning
Writing

110